3RD & 10

"Overcoming the Pitfalls of
Becoming a
College Football Player"

Dr. Roosevelt "Bug" Isom, Jr.

FORMER NCAA FOOTBALL PLAYER | SPEAKER | COLLEGE DIRECTOR

Dedication

I DEDICATE THIS book to every high school football player who has the aspiration to one day play the game they love on the college and professional levels. I want to also dedicate this book to the game of football, George P. Butler High School, Georgia Tech, my former coaches, and teammates! Lastly, I dedicate this book as I do with everything else to my Lord and Savior Jesus Christ for strengthening me with his glorious power so that I will have all the patience and endurance I need!

Table of Contents

Foreword

A FAMOUS CHINESE proverb states, "To know the road ahead, ask those coming back." In other words, if you want to know what to expect on your journey, take the time to learn from someone who has already been there. My friend, Dr. Roosevelt Isom Jr., has not only traveled the roads that you have begun to navigate, but he is also passionate about sharing the biggest lessons from that journey. Through *3rd & 10*, he provides a transparent account of both his triumphs and defeats as a Division I student-athlete.

Experience is truly the best teacher; however, not all learning experiences have to be your own. If you are committed to being the absolute best college student-athlete that you can be, I encourage you to read every word in this book with a receptive heart and an open mind. In doing so, you will have the opportunity to unlock your fullest potential in every aspect of your life.

In my travels to various schools around the country as a motivational speaker, I constantly encounter young athletes who become their own worst enemies in their pursuit of success. Instead of being intentional about the steps they should take to see long-term success both on and off the field, they rely solely on their athletic talent, expecting all of the right cards to simply fall into place. However, the reality is that only 2% of all high school football players actually make it to the NFL, and many football standouts are prepared for neither the academics of college nor for life once their football careers come to an end.

If you utilize the tools provided to you within the pages of this book, you can be confident that you will be able to successfully navigate the waters of being a college football player and overcome any pitfalls that commonly hold student-athletes back from achieving their goals. Dr. Isom is a living testimony of the ups and downs that can occur as a result of your decisions both in the classroom and on the football field. As someone who wants to see you succeed, I urge you to consciously carry each of these powerful lessons with you every day as you transition into college football.

Your future self will thank you for it.

Raven Magwood
International Speaker, Bestselling Author

Acknowledgments

I WOULD LIKE to acknowledge my wife and son for encouraging me and showing their love and support through this process. It's amazing how some of the most powerful lessons and accomplishments in life come from momentary setbacks. See, the writing of this book came at the expense of being laid off from my previous job. Despite this, my wife and son kept me encouraged and strong during this process. Therefore, I would like to say thank you, Lord, for my family and for guiding and motivating me to write this book so I could become transparent with my past as a college football player, to include being of help to others who pursue the same dream!

I would like to also acknowledge my newfound friend and second set of eyes, Ms. Raven Magwood. Raven is a well-known author and motivational speaker who has shown her unselfishness of time, opinion, and encouragement while assisting me with the completion of this book. I acknowledge and thank you, my friend!

Lastly, I would like to acknowledge and thank you, Lord, for being all powerful, all knowing, and always present for my care and protection!

In life, we all have a purpose; however, tapping into that purpose is the challenge. When we find that reason, we'll find our motivation and justification for which something is done or created. When this happens, we'll come to the realization of the intent or objective of that purpose. My purpose is and has always been to help others in some way, shape, or form. Presently, it is to help and serve as many high school football players as possible with their transition into playing college football.

I am prayerful and confident that my personal experiences as a former Division I Football Player and Senior Academic Leader will be sufficient to offer tips, advice, and truths that will serve as a guide/handbook for all high school football players during their transformation. God bless!

"Bug" Isom

"Rave Reviews"

My husband, my friend, my Godsend...I am so proud of the person you have become. Sharing your life experiences through your first (yes, first) book is nothing short of AWESOME. *3rd & 10* has so many lessons learned from your time playing the game of football that you so loved. Every young man that is fortunate enough to read this book, receive, and apply life instructions and lessons to their journey from high school football to the collegiate level will be blessed beyond measure. I pray for God's continued blessings upon you and our family and again I am so proud of you!

Always in Love,
Your wife, Barbara Isom

I am beyond blessed to have you as my dad, and extremely proud of you for writing this book! You taught me everything in this book, which led to me finding a college home and ultimately graduating with my bachelor's degree. This book is a must read for all high school juniors and seniors who plan on playing at the collegiate level. It is a major guide to choosing the best school for YOU based on your academic and athletic needs. In this book you will get a heads up regarding some of the obstacles you may face while being a student athlete, as well as lessons learned so you can hopefully take a better route. This book will also provide insight on the whole process and give you some knowledge about what to look for when choosing a school. All in all, I feel like this book will spread knowledge and help any and every college prospect with their decision when choosing a school.

Sincerely,
Your Son, Roosevelt Isom, III (Tre')
Former Wide Receiver (Savannah State University)

What's up, Bro?

I know it's early, but I wanted you to know that this book is a very real testimony that needs to be shared with so many who can relate. Your honesty and being up front with life events are those that most people can relate to. In this book, football and disappointments are used to illustrate your life and truths, but the book really tells a story of what life deals you when you don't prepare and stay ready. It tells a story of when we take our eyes off the prize (Jesus Christ), and start to think we're bigger than life (because folks make us feel that way when we're winning). Our God has a way of getting our attention and reminding us of who we are and whose we are. My life story parallels with yours and it has nothing to do with football, but what's interesting is that I speak with so many people (co-workers, church members, fraternity bros, family members, even my pastor friends) and I hear our story over and over; unfortunately, most won't share the true reality of their life of ups and downs with anyone outside their circle of close friends.

Thanks for sharing your testimony with so many who need to know that they too can tell their truths and reach out and help heal our land. I've read this book more than five times and I really really believe you have a story to share with not only athletes getting recruited to college, but to the world about "Overcoming Life's Pitfalls," and the world needs to hear it.

I've prayed this morning, with all sincerity and a few tears, that God would continue to bless you and your family and that He would bless this book in a way that it would release His Spirit of Love and Hope to all who read it. Continue to pray and meditate on how God wants you to do this (His) book (I don't know what this means, but God put it in my spirit). In closing, I leave this scripture with you 2 Chronicles 7:14 If my people, which are called by my name, shall humble themselves, and pray, and seek my face, and turn from their wicked ways; then will I hear from heaven, and will forgive their sin, and will heal their land.

Be blessed and keep your eyes on the prize. Love you much! I miss you Guys.

Mack A. Thomas, STS-C

As a long-time friend and colleague of this author, *3 &10--Overcoming the Pitfalls of Becoming a College Football Player* kept me on edge. It is an awesome read and highly recommended. The author depicts similarities between football, life, life after football, and how each is played in four quarters—not three, two, or one. Through personal life experiences, he repeatedly communicates, "It's not how you start, but how you finish." His journey exemplifies how the race has never been given to the swift, nor the strong, but to he who endures to the end. Thus, respect is earned, not given. Therefore, you too can finish strong because, like him, the only thing required is your very best!

Charles "Tight" Mack

I like the way you talked about personal experiences, good and bad, successes and failures, and mix that with the research from your dissertation, all the while providing focus, coaching, and direction to future young men who have the same goals and aspirations as you had coming out of high school. It's a concise read, but very impactful!

Dante Jones
College Roommate & Georgia Tech Teammate

Dr. Isom has written a terrific book that should be a must read for every high school and college student. He has brilliantly explained the importance of being a student athlete, and why education should always be the top priority for students who participate in athletics. Dr. Isom has graciously allowed his personal experiences to be used as a resource by student athletes all across America!

Kevin Ward
Vice President - Finance
100 Black Men of Augusta, Inc. (Mentoring Organization)

Love the strong sense of perseverance and the will to find one's purpose in your book! Plus, not just finding one's purpose but walking in it with confidence!

Cleve Pounds (Former Teammate)

3rd & 10 is an amazing book that is much needed for college athletes who are being recruited. This book is an easy read that all high school football players should read, whether or not they are planning on playing college ball. The lessons throughout each chapter are priceless! I am glad that someone is finally giving athletes the insight of looking at their academics in the overall recruiting process. As a teacher, I try to inform athletes that they are not going to succeed unless they can make it in the classroom. What's worse than not going to the school of your dreams due to academic shortcomings is getting there and not being able to make it in the classroom. It is refreshing to get a point of view from someone who has lived through the college football experience at the highest level and has the insight to tell about the ups and downs of recruitment, as well as the consequences of situations that happen once you get there. Dr. Isom has written an awesome book! If you are a parent of an athlete or an athlete, this is a MUST READ! Two thumbs up!

Chandra Magwood
Educator, Business Owner

When we talk about "Speaking Truth to Power," this book is the epitome of such. I could not think of a better way of conveying the obvious and sometimes the inevitable realities sometimes elude us. I truly believe that personal experiences are life's best teacher. "Bug," as I call him, has put together a must read for all student athletes. As a matter of fact, I think it should be incorporated in every college's curriculum that has any kind of sports programs. God has truly guided the heart and hands of this author. Job well done.

"Friend and Brother for Life" Tony Lewis

This book is perfect in so many ways. It is short, truthful, and informative. I have known Roosevelt all of his life. I have witnessed and been there for all of his highs and lows. It is rare that an African-American athlete that has come full circle lets you in on the journey through redemption. This book provides you the necessary steps that will ensure that you have a successful athletic college career. Roosevelt writes about his own successes and failures that put you right in the dorm rooms that he slept in while in college at Georgia Tech. It places you next to him when he falls from grace and has to face his father when he returns home from school. This raw encounter was a moment filled with intrigue and emotion.

I am super proud of this revealing life's lesson book. It is a book focused on making you a better decision-maker. The train is college recruitment for Division I minority athletes. The track is "student athlete." The station is at the end of the line. If you take this train and apply its principles, you will arrive at a "successful life." Read this book and embrace its lessons. You will be the better because of it!

Bill Diggs President
Mourning Family Foundation

So many young talented athletes are distracted by the glitz and glamour of competitive sports that they forget the real reason for attending college. Time and time again, star athletes veer off course and fail to understand that "the ball and the book" are inseparable. Dr. Isom's firsthand experiences are insightful, thoughtful, and carry a level of wisdom that those aspiring to be successful must pay attention to. I know firsthand how difficult it is to keep talented athletes focused on the game and academics. Every parent of a high school or college student athlete should read this testimony.

Glenn H. Andrews, Ed.S. School Principal (Retired)
Urban Educational Concepts, LLC
Setting the Stage for Successful Leadership

To the author as a brother, I'd like to say that your book and testimony of your life story is a must read for all young athletes. The correlation between sports and real life is what these young athletes need to hear. When I was growing up, we were told to always have a plan B in case plan A didn't work and to learn how to do more than one thing at a time. The point that you stress about the importance of working just as hard in the classroom as you do on the field to achieve your degree is a part of this book that should resonate in the hearts and minds of all athletes simply because there is life after sports. Also, to keep GOD in your life because HE knows what's best. I'm very proud of you on sharing a wealth of knowledge to all of these young athletes, friends, and family.

*Love, **Nathaniel Stephen (AKA) Big Bro***

Gridiron Blues

IT SEEMS LIKE it was just yesterday, warming up to play my last collegiate football game as a Georgia Tech Yellow Jacket against my rival the University of Georgia. In all my years playing against them, there was always a level of extreme excitement, but that night was different. I'm not sure if it was because it was a night game, cold, the dreariness of the rain, or the fact that this was my last college football game.

Sadly enough, I had become so caught up in the night life that I was thinking about where I was going after the game before the game even started. In some ways, over time, being caught up in the excitement of hanging out was like a drug without actually taking a drug. How about this—what do you think happened when I added that piece to the equation, along with alcohol? Well, I did, and had done for years off and on leading up to that point. Of course, I was as careful as possible because I/we were frequently tested, but that seed had been planted and was basically a way of life as a college football player!! Despite this, I regained focus while playing my last game and envisioned myself making one last play in front of family, friends, and fans. In retrospect, I had started the year off hurt, was later suspended for a game, had lost a step, and was totally unfocused on the game that I once loved.

Prior to the game, I can remember my receiver's coach telling me to stay ready to play, something I was optimistic about. Later, after the game started, I can clearly recollect early in the game a play, the play, in which the ball was thrown to a teammate that I was replaced by. I'm watching the play unfold as our quarterback drops back, my teammate running the same route I used to run day in and day out. He runs 10 yards and turns around, hands coming out as we've been taught, only to see the ball hit him right in the hands as he drops the ball! I'm thinking, *I should have been out there, because I would have made that play!*

At that very moment, I said YES, and yes, I said yes. Though it was politically incorrect to root against a teammate, I was quickly made aware that I still had a small fire burning on the inside, wanting to make one last play. As a result of my teammate's dropped ball, I began to have hope and began stretching, moving around a little, and even buttoning my chin strap. I began talking to myself, saying, "Okay, Bug, get ready, because your time is about to come," but it never did. I never played a down in my last college football game. So much early promise and expectations with nothing to show! I was like, damn! Having to watch an entire game from the sideline and for my parents, family, and friends to have to watch me watch the entire game from the sideline was very humiliating and shameful. In all my years of playing football from the 8th grade up, I can't remember a time when that ever happened!

After the game, I can remember being one of the first in the locker room. It felt like time was at a standstill, with me being the only one there with nothing but silence as my receiver's coach eventually walks towards me. He says "hang in there" and I said a few expletives to him as he finally walked away with me saying to myself "hang in there?" Hang in there for what and what am I hanging in there for? I'm thinking it's all over in the most devastating way. It felt like I had lost a family member! Family and friends were there to see me play my last game and I'm looking at guys playing my position that clearly didn't have the same talent as I once had as a wide receiver.

I truly hated that night, I hated the game, and seemingly everyone that was associated with it. I felt like someone had driven a stake into my heart and begun to just twist, and twist, and twist all the while saying that everything was going to be okay and to hang in there. I was thinking to myself, *where did the time go?* I was also wondering what happened to the high school standout that could run the 100-yard dash in 9.5 seconds and the 40 in 4.39 seconds. This was the same guy who was the 100- and 200-yard dash regional champion for two years in a row, to include champions in the 4X100 and 4X400 Relay Teams in the same years. What happened to that guy that was voted Male Athlete of the Year and held the longest run from scrimmage in school history and the second longest run in the county's history? Lastly, what happened to that guy who could run great routes and catch anything that came his way day in and day out?

It was like yesterday playing in my first high school football game as an excited 10th-grader. I played for Butler High School in Augusta Georgia and we were playing North Augusta High School out of South Carolina. You're talking PUMPED, I was pumped! Playing in front of my first sold-out crowd away from home and being watched by friends and family was a beautiful thing. Guess what? I didn't disappoint my friends, family, teammates, or coaches; however, I did disappoint the home team and crowd.

On that night, I showed out and handled my business similar to so many other occasions. See, back then there was no internet, just the morning and evening newspapers. So, after every game, we would read the local paper to see if my picture was taken or to see if an article was written describing my play from the night before. The next day, the paper's headline read, "Butler Rates High Grades!" In the body of the paper, it read, "Speedy sure-handed sophomore Roosevelt 'Bug' Isom was Mercer's target on the 85-yarder. Isom, who caught three passes for 127 yards, twice took the football away from a NA defender, and flashed his speed on the touchdown reception bursting past two pursuing NA backs!"

On another occasion, and one of my favorites, was when we played a school out of Douglas Georgia called Coffee County Trojans. These guys were good—and I mean really good, to include intimidating to some. We're talking nicknames like Pulpwood and Chainsaw, who were brothers. Despite the fierce competition, Pulpwood and I became good friends and played as teammates on the North/South Georgia All Star Game, with him later attending the University of Georgia with two of his teammates, becoming my teammates at Georgia Tech.

Though we lost the game with Coffee County topping us in a 28-13 win, I gained a lot of respect from players and coaches, with both wanting to talk and inquire after the game as to where I was going to play college football on the next level. I believe the attention was the result of doing something that normally didn't happen to that school, which was running for 95 yards from scrimmage for a touchdown on one of our first possessions.

The next day, the paper read, "Roosevelt 'Bug' Isom scored one touchdown on a 95-yard run – the longest run in school history, breaking the old of 86 yards by Kevin Belcher in 1976 against Westside. It's the second-longest scoring run from scrimmage since 1958 in county history, eclipsing all but Johnny

Raborn's 99-yard scoring run for Hephzibah against Washington-Wilkes in 1969." It seemed like every Saturday the newspaper printed something pertaining to my great play from the night before even if it was a small as, "Butler's Bug Isom (34) flies through the air to break up a pass" or stating "Mercer and his corps of receivers led by Bug Isom had begun to click late in the second quarter and the Bulldogs were breathing down Westside's neck after a pair of touchdowns." Just to name a few on so many nights!

But on that wet and dreary night, it was one of the worst nights and lowest points of my life. You know, in looking back, I brought it on myself and know that I drove that bus and no one else. But just when I felt it couldn't get any worse, it did. It was the end of the following quarter, and I can remember lying in bed in my dorm with no one in the room, hearing some of my teammates that were a part of my recruiting class congratulating each other on graduating with a degree, and some excited of the idea of being drafted by the NFL (National Football League) or at least getting a tryout. My news came in the form of a letter stating that I had been dismissed from school due to not maintaining an acceptable grade point average. As a result, I was required to sit out a quarter and ponder on what my next step would be. I mean, come on—I only had two quarters left to graduate, and this happened! Please understand that from the time I arrived at Georgia Tech, I immediately got caught up in the night life and the excitement of playing the game that I loved in the (ATL), Atlanta Georgia but not as caught up in my academics as I should have been.

So, I packed up all my things, got into my grey two-door '83 Cutlass, whitewall tires and all, and headed down I-20 East back to Augusta, Georgia. As I was driving home, it was one of the first times that I drove any amount of time without listening to music! I was riding, just shaking my head about the news I had just received, with a feeling of absolute numbness. You talk about a reality check—this was truly that, a reality check. I remember passing the Thomson Georgia sign and saying to myself, "Dang, I got another 30 minutes before I get home." I was wondering what the reception would be like from my mom and dad. Well, I knew I would get a hug and kiss from the queen of the house, but it was the king I was worried about! (LOL)

Like I expected, Mom greeted me with a hug and a kiss and asked if I was hungry. Pops didn't hug me but he did greet me and asked if I was okay. At that point, I felt much better and less anxious. The next couple of days and week seemed to go at the speed of a turtle but the following days and weeks began to move at warp speed and before I knew it, it was the weekend before I was to return to Georgia Tech one last time. I remember packing that weekend and Pops saying, "Okay, this is your last opportunity—so focus, son, do good, and call us when you arrive!" Once I arrived, the reality of how different things would be was soon apparent.

I was away from the team, rooming with a stranger, and not eating and jiving with the guys anymore. I literally felt out of place, alone, and unfocused without the realization and ramifications of what was going to happen if I didn't do well in my academics the following quarter. I also felt very detached and separated from all that I had previously known when it came to being a part of something special like my football family. Regardless, in knowing that this was my last opportunity, I should have become laser focused on the task at hand but I wasn't! I was just too far gone with my lack of interest in attending college and making the grades.

As a result, the following quarter, I officially flunked out of Georgia Tech! At this point I was saying to myself, "WOW, you gotta be FREAKIN' kidding me, you gotta be FREAKIN' kidding me!!" At that moment, everything was a blur, life seemed to be moving at lightning speed, and I was thinking what a waste and what a failure I had become. By now, I was feeling sorry for myself and not sure what my next step would be. Of course, now I had to share the news with my parents, all the while worrying about what others would think and how I would answer the many questions without lying. The funny thing is, everybody assumed I had graduated with a degree, and in my own way I was not truthful, because I just let them think what I knew hadn't happened. There's a saying, "The truth shall set you free!" I know the truth shall set you free, but I was like, "I'm not ready to be free," if you get my drift? Despite this, I still had to carry the load of always feeling weighted down because of being somewhat deceptive pertaining to my lack of achievement.

I felt really down and as though I had failed myself, friends, and family, but Psalms 30:5 says, "Weeping may endure for a night but joy cometh in the morning!" As a young man, I want you to know that it's not until you fail or perceive something to be negative that you'll really value the love of family, friends, and scriptures from the Holy Bible. As a result, I wasn't sure what to expect when I got home, but I soon found out. I found out that I had the greatest parents and friends who supported me regardless of my setback.

By this time, Pops, being true to form, shared with me that I had to get a job within the next couple of months. Once employed, I would be giving him $50 a week and if I was going to be hanging out to make sure I called him by midnight. This was to ensure I was coming home, because if I didn't, the screen door would be locked and I knew it wouldn't be a good idea to wake him up. See, back then only the grown folks had keys to the screen door, and if you knew Pops, you would appreciate that comment! True to form, I realized that things had changed and I had to become a man, get a job, and obey my parents' wishes—not some of the time, but all the time! Remember, always honor your mother, father, and grown folk!

The lesson in this piece is knowing that you will fall short in some areas and you will fail, but the key is getting back up and being true to yourself and others. Know that failure or setbacks are simply tools that will make you stronger, as well as the tools that will start the process of shaping and molding you into the strong, spiritual man you will become! I once read that "we should gladly suffer because we know that suffering helps us to endure, and endurance builds character, which gives us hope that will never disappoint us." Fast forwarding, not graduating from Georgia Tech to include playing the game of football taught me a plethora of life's lessons on endurance and building character, as well as what it means to persevere and trust in God.

Not graduating from the Georgia Institute of Technology was that failure and that negative lesson that motivated me to later obtain my Bachelor's Degree in Organizational Management from the historical Voorhees College, Master's of Science Degree in Management from Southern Wesleyan University, and later my Doctoral Degree in Organizational Leadership from the University of Phoenix. It's funny, if I can loosely use that term, how life will state your temporary residence in the valley of twist, turns, and ups and downs, not knowing that you will later accomplish bigger and better things at your new residence in faith through God's grace and mercy. I've learned over the years that there really isn't anything negative that transpires in your life—just simply life's lessons. Please know that what some deem as negative experiences are simply uncomfortable teachings, and what you may perceive as rejection is simply God's protection, so don't give up—learn from each situation, be a blessing to others, and keep it *MOVIN!*

In looking back, had I graduated from Georgia Tech, I probably wouldn't have felt the need or motivation to pursue other degrees, because I would have felt that a degree from Georgia Tech would have been good enough. Therefore, due to the disappointment of not graduating from the school that I loved and still love, I felt earning a doctoral degree and becoming *Dr. Isom* would be the only degree that would measure to the degree I would have earned had I graduated from Georgia Tech. Of course, based on societal standards, my doctoral degree weighs more than the bachelor's degree I would have obtained from Georgia Tech, but for me and through my journey, they are similar in value in my own little way. In essence and in a weird kind of way, I finally feel equal to those who graduated before me. Still, the idea of not completing what I started still somewhat haunts me to this day, so my message to you is, "Finish what you start when it comes to fulfilling your on-the-field and classroom responsibilities!"

My message to you is to complete what you start academically so you won't have any regrets. This also includes your commitment to the game of football, but remember that a college degree will provide you with the base needed to become successful in Corporate America, provided you are not fortunate to play professionally. The game of football will teach you many of life's lessons that will shape and mold you into the man you will become personally, physically, emotionally, professionally, and spiritually.

Because of such lessons, I felt the need to become transparent in the eyes of every high school football player who will be blessed to play the game of college football. My dream, like so many of yours, was to play professional football but there were and still are so many distractions, including what seemed to be a mirage of the real purpose of attending college. My goal is to continue sharing my story, provide you with advice on overcoming the pitfalls of becoming a college football player—specifically a Black college football player—and what to expect along the way. The start of your college football journey will begin when you get your first recruiting letter and visit. Therefore, if you want to understand the recruiting process, what to expect on recruiting trips, what to ask, and how to choose the college or university that's best for you, I urge you to keep reading, because you will be enlightened and amazed.

Recruiting 101

THE TERM *RECRUITING* refers to the overall process of attracting, shortlisting, selecting, and appointing suitable candidates, or in this case, high school football players like yourself, to play football for a college or university. During my high school years of playing football, I was honored and excited to be seriously recruited by so many top-notch colleges and universities. I can clearly remember eating lunch one day at my high school as my coach handed me letters of interest from Georgia Tech, University of South Carolina, Clemson, University of Georgia, Florida State, University of Tennessee, Mississippi State, Purdue, Furman, Georgia Southern, and as far out as UCLA, just to name a few.

The cool part was seeing the faces of my teammates and friends being excited about my perceived future success and commitment. The idea of knowing that college scouts would be present at our games evaluating my play on any given night was very exhilarating! Such an exciting time, but it didn't stop there; it went much deeper. I can remember on one of my recruiting trips, the head coach, my recruiter, my mom, dad, and of course yours truly took a tour of a university's campus. We ended up at that university's quiet and empty stadium when all of a sudden, the lights came on and over the intercom someone with a professional and charismatic voice shared, "And starting at wide receiver from Augusta Georgia, Roosevelt 'Bug' Isom!" followed by a thunderous cheer from an animated crowd of fans! That sent and still does send chills all over my body, and I was like, YES!!! At that moment, I felt invincible and was ready to play some big- time college football. I can promise you, at that moment academics was the last thing on my mind. With a little exaggeration, at that time and place had they suggested that I major in doing backward flips and designing shoes for lions, tigers, and bears, it would have been fine with me without question or concern because of the lure. Additionally, there was of course the night portion of the recruiting trips which consisted of going to parties, clubs, drinking, girls, coming home in the early-morning hours, and other things! I can promise you academics was the last thing on my mind, and not one athlete that played for that university talked academics the entire trip. It's simple— your recruiting trip is not designed for you to become excited about academics; it's designed for you to become excited about playing the game of football.

For you, the stakes may become much higher because nowadays sex, cash advances, the purchase of cars, homes, and even the placement of parents in better job opportunities may be your kryptonite or the thing that lures you to sign with that college or university. Today's recruiting tactics are far more advanced and tempting than they were 35-plus years ago. Today's recruiting efforts and landing the best football player is big business, so know that your recruiters and soon-to-be coaches have done their homework and already know your family's wants and needs. As a result, just know that the recruiting process is going to make you and your family feel like ROCK STARS that hit the lottery!

I felt the need to share those earlier examples because you have no idea of the length coaches, colleges, and universities will go through to get their guy, which could be you! I'm not asking you not to enjoy the moment but to just remember the two reasons why you are visiting that college or university. Those reasons are to graduate with a college degree and to play the game of football at the highest level. Therefore, the greatest thing about being recruited is that you can use the game as a platform to showcase your talents on the field but ultimately walk out with a college degree and zero debt!

During your recruiting experience, there will be no better feeling than knowing that you are wanted—and in your case, by some of the top colleges and universities in the country. To bring that point home, and if I may use a comparison, it's kind of like the prettiest girl at your school telling her friend to tell her friend to tell you that she likes you. As a result, you begin receiving letters, text messages, and calls from that girl and the two of you begin talking and going out on dates. Just when you start to have feelings for her and are about to commit to only seeing her, you meet another pretty girl from another school that's just as pretty but drives a better-looking car.

At the present, because you're feeling good about yourself (LOL), you believe you have the best of both worlds because of all the sudden attention, but let's go one step further. You indeed meet a third girl who is just as attractive as the previous two, drives an even nicer car, and you find that her parents are rich. My point is, the recruiting process is very similar in that it's an ongoing cycle of the next college or university sharing how good they are, how much better they are compared to the next, and what they can and will do for you above the others!

As a matter of fact, because you will be blessed to be recruited by so many colleges, you may find yourself becoming confused and overwhelmed about where to attend because they'll all sound so good and tempting. As a result, the recruiting process may go from being fun to not so fun. It's even possible that you may begin to shy away from a few, so here's how to resolve that perceived issue.

In looking back at the examples of the girls, addressing their looks, their cars, and their money were the ingredients that attracted you and made you feel like you had it going on, right? Think about it; all of the aforementioned points are simply materialistic. Being with someone who's pretty, drives a nice car, and has money is good, but it doesn't mean she's the right one for you. You'll have to ask yourself, "What things do I like to do and talk about? Do we come from similar backgrounds? Is she caring and nice or is she selfish and arrogant? Does she listen or does she like to talk all the time?" My point is, you'll tend to be the happiest with someone with whom you have the most in common, one who listens, and one that you feel the most comfortable with.

Moving forward, I want you to ask yourself those same questions when it comes to being recruited, because what you'll find is that things will be very similar in nature during this process. What you'll find is that most if not all colleges/ universities will shine with things that are materialistic. What I mean by materialistic is the state-of-the-art locker rooms, the state-of-the-art weight rooms and sound systems, your roomy dorm room, the many trophies and championships, not to mention the many pics of former players who played professionally. All these things are great selling points and valid from a football point of view, but what about the school's environment and class offerings, as well as graduation rates of football players? Consider this, if all of the aforementioned materialistic stuff was not shown or talked about, would you attend? Would you be interested?

The same question will apply during your recruiting process with these schools. The college or university that's recruiting you will promote their facility as well as the fact that you'll have a good chance to start at your position to include winning National Championships if you come to that school. Similar to the previous question, is that school really a good fit for you? What if you love computers and that school doesn't offer a major in computers? What if you love biology but that school doesn't have a credible biology program? What if you like homeland security or cyber work but that school doesn't offer those majors—do you think you should or do you still want to go? Do you think it would be logical to commit to that school? Isn't it about being with the one that's truly the right fit for you on and off the field? I'll let you answer that question, but it's worth thinking about.

My point is, don't let the materialistic STUFF cloud your mindset on the real reason and objective of attending college, which is to graduate with a college degree. Let's go a step further—remember the pretty girl you met that liked to talk but didn't listen? The same may apply during your recruiting process. Because you are an exceptional football player, there will be a lot of talking and suggestions made by that college or university on their behalf and not yours. Their objective is to put you in the mindset of where they want you to be during that visit. Remember, your main objective is to complete your college education, as well as performing at a high level on the football field. So, ask yourself and that university what types of majors are offered, and then take a snapshot of the city to see if the city fits you. Is the city too big or too small? If you went to school in New York, attending a school in Atlanta or California won't be an issue for you. But if you're from a population of 1000 people, going to a school in a major city might become an issue.

Just know that recruiting represents one of the major components that ensures a college or university gets the best of the best of high school football players. With that being said, know that you're being recruited not because you're great in the classroom but because you're great on the football field. Just to prove my point that this process hasn't changed in the last 35-plus years, digest this occurrence. I can recollect several years ago I was on a recruiting trip with my son at a widely known top five football university that invited him to one of their camps.

As my son was running routes and preparing for one on one drills, a man walked up to me and introduced himself. Because I was representing Georgia Tech with a hat and shirt, something I probably shouldn't have done, I was asked if I played there, and of course I stated with pride that I did, and the years. I was then asked which one was my son and as I pointed him out, the man made the comment that he had really good size and hands and that particular university could use a big wide receiver like him.

I followed with a comment pertaining to a few of his accomplishments on the field without being braggadocious and followed with my proudest comment, which was my son's accomplishments in the classroom, to include his academic rankings among his senior class. I was expecting a *that's great, awesome job, academics is important*, or even a *fake high five*, but instead I got the most unexpected response. That man looked me straight in my eyes and said with pride, "Oh, that doesn't apply here; we're recruiting to win football games!"

That comment was a *WOW* moment for me, because the idea of recruiting smart football players didn't seem to be the norm or important to this university.

Though the coaches and staff members of that SEC school (whoops) would probably disagree with this man's comment, this man stated that he comes to these open camps every year and knows the coaches personally. The forwardness and bluntness of that comment really took me aback! I know that playing in front of thousands of fans, catching touchdowns, winning the conference, and hopefully a National Championship is what initially comes to mind and what all colleges and universities will sell to a soon-to-be recruit like you. Despite that, just do me a favor—while being recruited, ask about graduation rates among football players. As shared and quoted by a well-known former college coach, "I was hired to win football games, not to graduate football players." He further stated, "If I don't win games, I won't have a job!"

The goal of every coach is to recruit and sign the best athletes and football players. The recruiting process is geared to make you and family believe you are their number one interest of that college or university. They'll do this by keeping your mind focused on what can be done on the football field and not in the classroom. But please understand that what is being said to you will probably be said to every other recruit that comes in the following week and the weeks after. Yes, the conversation of academics will be mentioned, but not at the same magnitude and with the same excitement as what can be done on the football field. Recruiters and coaches will go as far as to paint a picture of your potential as a future *NFL Great*, with little regard for sharing your potential for being *Great* in the classroom, the importance of obtaining a college degree, or the fact that only 2% will make it to the professional level.

I can clearly remember on several occasions while on re-cruiting trips, a very high percentage of my conversations with coaches and alumni pertained to football and not academics. However, much of the conversation that I would hear toward football players from other nationalities was more related to aca-demics as well as football. It didn't dawn on me until thirty-five years later how the dream of playing professional football and the reality of only 2% of college football players making it to the NFL was implanted in the minds of all of us, but just in different ways.

For example, that same 2% that seek to make it to the pro-fessional ranks means for every 200 NCAA football players, only four will ever play in the NFL. Yes, you read that right! To use an even higher and more realistic number involving Division 1, 2, & 3 Collegiate programs, for every 10,000 football players, only 200 of you will make it to the next level. Lastly and more importantly, there are 32 teams in the NFL and only seven rounds for teams to choose the player of their choice. You do the math! Regardless of the deck being stacked against you, know that you have every opportunity to become one of the 2% if you recognize the system as well as learning how to play the game of football at very high level.

In looking back, it wasn't necessarily the fault of coaches for talking only football, because certain cultures in our so-ciety mainly talk sports, too. From the standpoint of a Black football player, society, our family, and friends are implant-ing in most minds the thought of becoming a college football star and one day a professional star. In many cases, this is the result because this is the only way many can see themselves be-coming financially stable. Whereas, from the standpoint of non-Black football players, society, family, and friends are stressing the importance of a good education and how their education will play a vital role in their future success, both personally and professionally.

This piece really needs to be shared, because we've already discussed the fact that only 2% of college football players will play professionally. So, wouldn't it be wise for you to ask questions pertaining to the academic piece while being recruited, regardless of whether you're Black or White? Please be aware that some of the colleges and universities that will be recruiting you possess extremely poor graduation rates among certain nationalities of football players, specifically Black football players. To bring the point home, there was an earlier study that revealed staggering comparisons proving that Black football players are graduating at significantly lower rates than their White counterparts. I share this because as a former Black Division 1 football player, in almost every case while being recruited, very little time was spent on behalf of academics compared to hanging out, talking football, and meeting future teammates. The majority of your time will be spent with other existing football players, having lots of fun and hearing everything a young teenage high school football player wants to hear.

During your recruiting visit, you and your family will stay in some of the nicest five-star hotels, eat some of the most delicious meals, and become showered by continuous amounts of attention that's perfectly orchestrated toward you and your entire family, to convince you to play football for that college or university. Oh yeah—your parents will get the full treatment too, and yes, it's going to be hard not to get caught up in all the attention, because in some ways your parents are being recruited too!

Regardless, when the opportunity arises for talks pertaining to academics, don't be shy; question the variety of majors offered and the work load for each. Also, based on the majors offered, ask or research how that major fits in today's society and whether it's even a suitable or a realistic major for future job opportunities. Know that it's your right as a football player being recruited to inquire or even suggest what major best fits you, versus your coach or advisor telling you what they think fits you. Again, I can't stress this enough, because most Black football players are seemingly placed in similar, less challenging, or the same majors compared to players of other nationalities. The term associated with this type of grouping is called *academic clustering*. *Academic clustering* is the process of placing the majority of one ethnic group of athletes into one or two groups of majors, usually perceived as the easiest of majors.

In many cases, based on your high school GPA (Grade Point Average), colleges and universities will suggest or be so bold to tell you what would be a good major for you without asking. This is somewhat ludicrous, because in the majority of cases, what you would like to become or the subjects you like are dismissed for a major that will keep you eligible to play, only to have your hardest classes left to complete at the end of your football career. Colleges and universities will do this because they have already assured your academic workload, and in some cases will discourage you from taking classes associated with a more challenging major. Please understand that your future schooling is already mapped to ensure you will be eligible to play four years of football. Here's another tip: be mindful that staying eligible for four years doesn't mean that you will be closer to graduating, because in most cases, you will be left with the hardest of courses to complete, which is the main reason why most athletes/football players don't graduate after their eligibility is over.

Because academic clustering has been proven and prevalent among colleges and universities, it is imperative that you and your parents become aware of this term. Don't be afraid to ask the tough questions that may affect your academic future, to include making suggestions on an academic major that best suits who you want to become and what you want to do professionally after your college football career is over.

For the third or fourth time, the reality is that only 2% of college football players make it to the NFL. This is not to discourage you but to speak candidly the seriousness of maintaining a good balance on the field and in the classroom. Once you complete your last game of eligibility, you will basically serve no purpose or be of no use to that respective college or university from an athletic point of view. The question will then be to yourself, *what will I do now? Will I walk out with a college degree, or will I return home believing it was all just a dream that came and passed?* I believe you will be that person that will complete what you started, graduate with a college degree, and play professionally, because I have that kind of faith in you! Why can't we have it all, right?

At the end of the day, the recruiting process will be the process that will kick start your mind on painting a picture of dreams versus reality. It will also become the process that starts your mental and physical preparation for what needs to be done to ensure those dreams do become a reality. So, what's the discrepancy between the two? Well, I'm about to break down the difference, so keep reading and tell me what you think!

Dreams vs Reality

DREAMS CAN BE defined as a series of thoughts, images, or emotions occurring during sleep; a visionary creation of the imagination and state of mind marked by obstruction of release from reality; a strongly desired goal or purpose. On the other hand, reality can be defined as the world or state of things as they actually exist; the state of quality of having existence or substance.

When it comes to playing college football or one day playing professionally, those things could become both a dream and a reality. Almost every young man that plays college football dreams or should dream of playing at the next level--I know I did! I had it all planned. It was kind of ironic that my junior high school, high school, and college colors at that time were black and gold. Therefore, you couldn't have told me that I wouldn't be drafted and play for either the Pittsburgh Steelers or the New Orleans Saints due to their colors also being black and gold. That was my dream and coming out of high school with all the attention I was receiving across the nation had me believing this was a dream that would one day become a reality.

The reality for me was that I didn't make it to the (NFL) National Football League and was **NOT** one of the 2% of college football players who've accomplished that dream. Do

I believe you can make your dreams become a reality? Yes, I do! Do I believe you have the intestinal fortitude to make your dreams become a reality? Yes, I do! Do I believe you will have the work ethic and discipline to make your dreams become a reality? Yes, I do!

The question is, do you believe? If you do believe, know that you will have to go above and beyond the call of duty to reach your dreams! As the great Hall of Famer Jerry Rice expressed, "Today I will do what others won't, so that tomorrow I can accomplish what others can't!" What Jerry Rice is saying is that in order to be the best, you'll have to train mentally and physically in ways that others wouldn't or don't want to. He's also saying that you'll have to push yourself to limits unheard of in order to become a part of the 2% that make it professionally. In a perfect world, we would all be accomplished in reaching all of our dreams, but we wouldn't know what it means to work hard, persevere, or possess the faith that our dreams will one day become a reality.

On the other hand, sometimes no matter how hard we work and no matter how bad we want something, sometimes God has other plans for our lives. This means that some of our dreams don't become realities. In my case, I broke my collar bone twice on the same side in my years of playing for Tech, which at that time were season-ending injuries. I had a healthy, not so productive 3rd year, but started in the All-American Bowl beating Michigan State for one of Georgia Tech's first bowl games in some time. Finally, in my last year, I had very high expectations but suffered a high ankle sprain to start the season, never to be physically or mentally healthy for the rest of the year.

The reality pertaining to the game of college football is next man up. In the minds of coaches, "Are you the best guy that can help win football games?" This is important because winning games constitutes the future of all coaches, so I get it! In looking at the majority of most rosters and starting lineups of colleges and universities, you'll see that they list the best of the best players—this list has a very high percentage of a certain nationality, which are young Black men, but that same nationality of Blacks also has the lowest rate of success when it comes to graduating with a college degree. That's reality!

Studies have shown that retention rates among Black football players are much lower than their White counterparts. For example, a study less than ten years ago stated that 100% of White football players who attended an SEC (South Eastern Conference) University completed their schooling, compared to less than 50% of their Black counterparts. Studies have also shown that Black football players are prepared for personal readiness on the football field but not in the classroom or for future professions. The aforementioned statistics go back to the questions I shared earlier pertaining to what I want you to ask during your recruiting visit! Just from this one statistic, can you now see the importance of asking the right questions, especially if you are a Black football player? Another fact suggests that the lack of degree attainment is an experience that under-prepares student athletes to be academically and personally ready to assume positions within the mainstream business community after college and following the exhaustion of potential in their sports career. What does this mean? This basically means that in the eyes of Corporate America, you are not prepared to hold leadership positions if you don't possess a college degree!

Here's another reality—coaches are paid millions and millions of dollars to win games, not to graduate students. As a high school football player, I want you to understand that you are not being recruited because you're smart, you're being recruited because you play the game of football at an exceptionally high level. There are quotes by some very well-known college coaches who have publicly made the aforementioned statements. I want you to recognize that in the minds of most if not all coaches, they stand by the motto that "winning on the football field comes first and winning in the classroom comes second."

To prove this point, I can clearly remember in my last year one of my coaches saying, "Academics comes first," holding up two fingers and later stating, "Football comes second," but holding up one finger. Though the statement was verbally correct, the nonverbal cues and expectations were, are, and will always be what is really correct and expected. Making such a statement in that manner made crystal clear the real intentions of what's most important. Scholars have argued that an athlete's increased attention to athletics and lack of focus on academics contributes to low college-graduation rates. I want you to understand that colleges expect to win with great athletes and not great students. As shared earlier, some coaches may devalue your academic success as a student-athlete, which means they may attempt to enroll you in a less-demanding course and choose a major held in LOW standing! To add, coaches may also instruct you to take courses from student-athlete-friendly faculty who will provide you with special consideration in the classroom. This is reality!

Be aware that in institutions where much emphasis is placed on winning on the field and not in the classroom, you could become academically unprepared to compete for jobs in society after college and following your college football career. As recently as ten years ago, an ACC (Atlantic Coast Conference) team was convicted of fraud involving sixty-one student-athletes.

As a result, it was found that student-athletes from that university received improper assistance from a learning specialist—tutors within that university's Academic Support Service Department.

My hope is that when you're going through the recruiting process, you keep these things in mind. Do your homework pertaining to past fraud and graduation rates of different races and nationalities, particularly yours at that particular college or university. This will ensure that as a football player you will know the facts and increase your odds of graduating with a college degree. Regardless, know that not initially graduating with a college degree isn't the end of the world; it's just the end of one of the many chapters that will be applied to your life. With that being said, we have four possible scenarios! First, you graduate with a college degree, but you don't play professional football! Second, you graduate with a college degree and you're blessed to play professional football! Third, you don't graduate with a college degree, but you're blessed to play professional football! Fourth, you don't graduate with a college degree, and you're not blessed to play professional football.

Let's look at each. If you graduate with a degree but aren't fortunate enough to play professionally, that is still a blessing. With that being the case, my first words to you will be, "Congratulations, young man! So proud of you!" That'll mean that you've accomplished the main goal of attending college and graduating with a degree. For this, you would have shown and proven that society believes that you are ready for Corporate America to become a manager, CEO, or owner of any business you so see fit! If you graduate with a degree and blessed to play professionally, it means that you have achieved the best of both worlds and your dreams have become a reality. Now, you'll have access to exceptional financial advice on how to save and invest from your NFL earnings into a business that ties into the degree you have already obtained. Again, this will warrant a "Congrats, young man, for a super job of achieving your dreams." If you don't graduate but are fortunate enough to play professionally, that is still a good deal because you can always account for the off season to accomplish your goal of completing your college degree. You wouldn't be the first or the last to complete your degree in this manner. Again, a "Job well done!" will be in order! Lastly, if you don't complete your degree and are not fortunate enough to play professionally, that isn't the end of the world either. Not achieving either means that you are now qualified to minister to others regarding what it takes to succeed and persevere, as I did and still am doing. I am a living example of what can be achieved as a result of academic and professional setbacks, if you put your mind to it. The same drive I had and have is the same drive I can see in you, so whatever scenario you're faced with, know that anything is possible!

To prove my point, tell me if you recognize any of these names: Larry Fitzgerald, Shaquille O'Neal, Emmitt Smith, and Bo Jackson, just to name a few. The aforementioned professional athletes went back to school and obtained their college degrees after their professional careers started. These men understood the importance of a college degree and how finishing what you start is so very important. For example, Larry Fitzgerald played college football for the University of Pittsburgh and later was drafted by the Arizona Cardinals as a wide receiver. Before his mom's passing in 2003, he promised his mother that he would go back to school and obtain his bachelor's degree. In 2016, he accomplished that goal. Larry later shared in an interview that he saved the recording of his mother's voice on their answering machine so he could always hear her voice. Later, in a touching tribute, there's a commercial that shows him calling his mother and leaving a message sharing that he fulfilled his promise by obtaining a college degree and telling her that he loves her!

What about your Boy Shaquille O'Neal? Shaq played college basketball for the LSU Tigers and later was drafted by the Orlando Magic and later played with five more professional teams, winning multiple NBA championships. Shaq, like so many others, understood the importance of a college degree. Similar to Larry Fitzgerald, he too made a promise to his mother that he would obtain a college degree. As a result, he not only obtained his bachelor's and master's degrees but later obtained a doctorate in education from Barry University, a private Catholic institution in Florida.

When it came to Hall of Famer Emmitt Smith, he also knew he wanted to later accomplish the goal of one day obtaining a college degree. Smith played his collegiate football career at the University of Florida and later won multiple Super Bowls with the Dallas Cowboys and was eventually inducted into the Pro Football Hall of Fame. Smith returned to the University of Florida six years after he left college, graduating with a bachelor's degree in Health and Human Performances. Now, Emmitt Smith is a very prosperous businessman in the Dallas, Texas area, where he has become diverse in his business ventures, bringing positive change to communities as a successful and socially responsible developer.

Lastly, let's look at one of the most multi-talented athletes of all time, the great Bo Jackson. For those of you who didn't know, but "Bo Knows!" Bo Jackson was the eighth of ten kids, three of whom stutter – Bo, as well as two of his sisters. According to a profile shared, Bo developed a stutter as a child and became extremely self-conscious about it. He avoided raising his hand in class, for fear of being made fun of by the other students. Despite this, Bo worked hard and was recruited as a running back and played the outfield for the Auburn Tigers baseball team. Bo was later drafted by the Raiders and became a two-sport professional athlete, playing outfield for the Kansas City Royals, something that was unheard-of from a professional athlete's standpoint! Despite his success on the field, Bo never forgot the promise he also made to his mother that he would obtain a college degree, which he later did in 1995 from Auburn University. Like Bo, you may possess some shortcomings, but know that it doesn't have to stop you from achieving your dreams.

These are just a few examples of some of the greatest athletes of all time who did not initially graduate from college. Yet, these men dug deep from within and accomplished goals in their sports as well as away from their sports against many odds. These men could have said to themselves, "I have enough money, so why a college degree?" They could have listened to their critics or haters of being classified as simply dumb jocks but they didn't. So, my question to you is, are you going to dig deep from within when you're faced with adversity? Who will you make your promise to when it comes to achieving your college degree, and who are you listening to? WOW, what a great time to have inquired, because the next chapter is asking the same question: "Who Are You Listening To?" Well, let's see!

Who Are You Listening To?

PERSONAL AND PROFESSIONAL influences come in many different forms, whether it's family, your local church, the community, society, or even our laws and regulations. In most cases, depending on background, a football player such as yourself may be influenced by family and the community on one day seeing you play professional football and less of an influence on seeing you graduate with a college degree.

Case in point: I can remember as a young child playing football in my old neighborhood. We use to play touch football in the streets, which was the length of one light pole to the next. There was also a cable line that hung low that went from one side of the street to the other. Since we didn't have an actual goal post, we used that cable line as our goal post where we would hold and kick footballs as extra points. In order to play, we would have to ask our neighbors to move their cars into their driveways so we could use the entire street. As I would fake, jump, catch balls, and run for touchdowns, I would hear some saying, "Boy, you going to the pros." Even at such an early age, the thought of playing professionally was always on my mind and shared by friends and family.

If I wasn't playing football, I was watching it on TV. At that time, the Miami Dolphins was my favorite team. Because

I loved them so much, my father bought me a Miami Dolphins football uniform, a sweater, a letterman jacket, socks, hat, mittens, a pajama top and pants. Anything dealing with football and the Dolphins had my attention, so yes, I can honestly say I was listening and believing the hype from friends and family. Please note that most well-known rich African-American males during that time played a professional sport. Conversely, men who were Caucasian were doctors, lawyers, or movie stars. Because my friends and I were always playing some type of sport, it was the norm to believe this would be the chosen path if we wanted to have a good life. The ironic part of this story is that my neighborhood was middle class and my friends and I had parents who had very good jobs and held high positions. Despite this, it never crossed my mind to want to do the same type of work. My mindset was on playing a professional sport and getting good grades.

On the other hand, it's been researched and proven that football players that come from low-income or one-parent homes, or from homes whose parents do not possess a college degree, are less likely to encourage working hard in the classroom but more likely to encourage working hard on the football field. The dream or idea of playing professional football and to one day provide financial freedom and all of the materialistic things money can buy somehow clouds the minds of most players, because this is what they're listening to. For a very small few, playing professional football will happen, and that will be an *awesome* day. For those who may not get that chance, you will have to ask yourself, "What happens now?" This same question should be asked of oneself prior to starting your college career. Take the time to ask yourself, "Who am I listening to, and what will happen if I don't become a professional football player or obtain a college degree? Further, what kinds of jobs will I be able to get with only a high school diploma?" Just something to think about!

You must understand that as a college football player you'll have to frequently study your academics, and even if you have a great supporting cast, that still doesn't guarantee success in the classroom. I'm a prime example, because I came from a middle-class family that stressed academics. My father was a retired master sergeant in the army, my mother is a retired school teacher, and both of my sisters possess college degrees. Still, I allowed outside influences to cloud my thinking, attitude, and preparation toward my college academics—so don't let this be you. I'm sharing this with you because it's very easy to become distracted. Remember, student-athletes from low-income or one-parent homes are more susceptible to fail in the classroom. Even if you are an athlete coming from a middle-class or upper-class family, that doesn't eliminate being susceptible to failure too.

The most influential people and things leading to your college career will consists of your family, friends, and your environment. These influences will play a vital role in your maturity toward the game of football and academics, because the same people and things will be the very people and things that you will be listening to. Your influences are important, because there may be one influence that dictates whether you graduate or not. Know that your parents' participation will become very important and key to your scholastic and athletic development.

When you are a football player who comes from a single-parent family, housed in a small home with several siblings, your focus is less on academics, but more on what you do best, which is playing the game of football. Sometimes it seems on the surface that players who come from these types of backgrounds are the hungriest for professional success compared to those who come from a balanced home. I would suggest that such a hunger is the result of feeling that there's no alternative to what one can envision seeing themselves doing aside from playing the game of football.

In looking back, I had a hunger, but not that dire hunger of feeling as though there was no life after football and that playing the game was all I could do. I was always taught, saw, and realized that I had options while playing the game. So, I'll ask you as a football player—what are your options, if any? If you don't have any options, start the process of addressing what those options and goals could become. If you do have goals aside from wanting to play professional football, I'd suggest using your future school's scholarship to acquire the necessary components needed to reaching your off-field goals. Moving forward, know that you have options, and please ensure that you are listening to the right people and ignoring the negative.

In the following chapter, I'm sharing the most powerful of all truths, the truth pertaining to what's most important in the eyes of coaches, the truth related to graduation rates of football players, specifically Black football players from the colleges and universities that will be recruiting you, as well as how learned experiences on and off the field will assist you in your future endeavors! With that being said, if you want to know the truth, keep reading, because this next chapter will blow you away!

The Truth Shall Set You Free

FIRST THINGS FIRST: know that the truth is always a good thing despite your feelings afterwards; and the truth at least gives you a clear mind to make good future decisions. Accordingly, this chapter will provide you with some truths pertaining to graduation rates of football players, the lack of retention rates of Black football players compared to their White counterparts, and the main goal of college coaches. Furthermore, this chapter will expound on the many factors that will attribute to your mental development, to include firsthand quotes from Black former NCAA football players who did not graduate with a college degree. Lastly, this chapter will provide you with knowledge pertaining to learned experiences on and off the football field and how those learned experiences may help you during and after your college football journey. This is powerful information because not only are you hearing firsthand accounts of my learned experiences, but you'll hear from a host of other former players pertaining to their learned experiences as former college football players. Understand that the same do's and don'ts, to include firsthand accounts of others' learned experiences, will be the very things that will assist you in making the right choice on where you should or should not attend college to play football. So, let's dive in and start with you as a future college student-athlete.

It's been proven that roughly 65% of Division I student-athletes, individuals soon to be like you, who began a four-year college or university program graduated with a degree. If you're recruited by Division I colleges or universities, know that they are generally the most powerful in athletic sports because they possess the greatest number of sports teams and team members that receive the largest amounts of financial support and possess the most competitive of sports programs in the NCAA. So, what does this mean? This means that top Division I programs have more than just football, baseball, and basketball teams and in almost all cases carry more players than Division II or Division III colleges. This also means that millions and millions of dollars are invested in these schools to gain fans by winning games and championships. Therefore, it will be imperative that you perform at the highest level!

Therefore, Division I schools need to profit millions of dollars yearly to support such programs. When you win, your fans and alumni will come to see you play and when you're not winning, they stay home. Still, the retention rates—or should I say graduation rates—of student-athletes attending Division I colleges remain very low. More noteworthy are the low retention rates of Division I student-athletes who are Black, so please pay attention, and let's address this issue.

Let's think about it—there's an issue when only 56% of Black student- athletes graduate from college, and fewer than 50% of Black college football players leave post-secondary institutions with a degree. This is why in my earlier chapters I'm stressing that as a Black football player, or any player, you need to inquire about the graduation rates of football players from the schools that are recruiting you. You have to make this a vital piece of your visit during your recruiting process, because student-athletes are struggling to earn college degrees, and Black student-athletes are underperforming academically compared to the majority of the population. If you are a non-Black football player, you still need to inquire, because you're playing the same game and going through the same process. As stated earlier, the message of football players being personally ready on the football field and not in the classroom may be the reason for low graduation rates. Again, wouldn't you as a football player, specifically a Black football player, see this as an issue?

So now, your question to me may be, how do you become personally ready for the classroom? Well, I'm glad you asked! You start by putting in the time studying like you would preparing for a football game. You start by working out your brain along with other parts of the body. Therefore, I want you to seek help when needed from teachers or tutors pertaining to your weakest subject. I also want you to establish friendships with students who don't necessarily play sports but may be able to help when needed. Further, I ask that you become a part of different organizations within your school so you'll have other groups of friends to reach out to. Lastly and most importantly, I don't want you to become afraid or feel inferior because you're asking for help. Asking for help doesn't make you weak; asking for help makes you strong, and it shows your maturity as a young man! Not only will it show your maturity as a young man, but it will put you in the percentage of football players who do graduate compared to those who don't.

To prove my point, some years ago it was discovered that 100% of White football players' who attended an SEC University completed schooling compared to less than 50% of their Black counterparts. Another university that's a member of the Big 12 Conference was another college which had a 59% graduation rate among White football players and only 34% among Black players. So, if you are a high school football player, specifically a Black high school football player that's fortunate enough to be recruited by such powerhouse schools, wouldn't you want to know what those percentages are as well as what is being done to ensure all football players graduate with a college degree? Your answer should be an emphatic YES! I just wondered, for those that didn't graduate, whether they took the advice that I'm now offering to you. At the end of the day, regardless of the schools recruiting you and regardless of your race, I am confident that you'll do the right thing by asking the aforementioned questions as well as seeking help when needed!

So how does all of this relate? Earlier I spoke of the importance of obtaining a degree, because it shows that you are prepared regardless of the profession. Well, the same applies here, because the lack of degree attainment is an experience that underprepares you to be academically or personally ready to assume positions within the business community after college and following your college football career. The lack of degree attainment to include different degree levels plays a major role with one's future annual salary. For example, a few years ago it was researched and proven that the average salary for a high school graduate was $17,299. The average salary for a graduate earning a bachelor's degree was $48,351. Notably, the average salary for a graduate earning a master's degree was $53,000, and the average salary for a graduate earning a doctoral degree was $72,000.

To put it plainly, if you graduate with a college degree, you are considered prepared for leadership positions, which will provide a higher income. If you don't graduate with a college degree, you'll be viewed as not prepared, making less than a college graduate. Of the two, which one would you like to become considered as—prepared or not prepared? If you said prepared, as I expected, then you'll need to take the steps shared earlier when it comes to your academic preparation. By doing so, you are keeping your eyes on the prize of graduating with a college degree!

When it comes to coaches, they expect to win with great football players and not great students. Again, you're being recruited because you're good on the football field and not necessarily because you're good in the classroom.

Therefore, you need to understand that some coaches may devalue your academic success as they instruct you to enroll in less-demanding courses and choose majors held in low standing. When I say low standing, I'm speaking of majors that are the easiest, compared to others that aren't associated with the highest of post-schooling paying jobs. When you hear easiest, I know what you're thinking. You're thinking, "Why not easy classes?"

Well, more than likely, the easiest of classes and majors will probably be the least paying when it comes to jobs related to that major when you graduate. To go a step further, coaches may also instruct you to take courses from student- athlete-friendly faculty who provide student-athletes with special consideration in the classroom. Therefore, you want to become aware of the institutions where much emphasis is placed on sports achievement in comparison to academic achievement. Because of such institutions, many student-athletes become academically unprepared to compete for jobs in society after college and following the end of often short-lived sports careers, something we don't want to happen to you! The more powerful and well known the school, the more that school will ensure your football eligibility so you can compete on the football field.

For example, past Division I athletes participating in football have been associated with academic violations such as obtaining special privileges from academic tutors, receiving credit for deficient student assignments, and cheating on examinations. Case in point—remember that ACC college football scandal I was telling you about before? Does this mean that an ACC university is a bad school? That's for you to decide! Does this mean they got caught? The answer is an astounding yes! If you're recruited by a school who's been caught for academic or recruiting violations, affirm their present status, see what has been done since the violation, and validate that these issues or violations are being addressed and resolved.

As a high school football player and soon-to-be collegiate football player, I don't want you to become naïve as to how you will be viewed as an individual. Many people inside and outside the college community have formed or will form pessimistic attitudes and stereotypes towards you as a college football player, particularly as a Black college football player. These same pessimistic attitudes are the attitudes that may negatively affect you when your college football career is over, to include when it's time for you to seek leadership positions for future job opportunities. Again, ignore and dismiss these beliefs. What this basically means is that in the eyes of many, Black football players are primarily viewed as dumb jocks or not intelligent and only good for one thing, and that's playing the game of football at the highest level on Saturdays.

Did you know that the largest and most visible groups of Black student- athletes is the group of Division I football players? Yet this same group is also the group with the lowest graduation rates. What's disheartening is although there have been years of discussion concerning the reasons for such academic underperformance and low graduation rates, there have been few efforts to understand why the problem exists from the Black student-athletes' perspective. For this reason, while in pursuit of my doctoral degree, I conducted a study of roughly twenty Black former college football players who did not graduate from their respective college, to gain knowledge of their views and lived experiences as college football players.

In speaking with several Black former Division I football players pertaining to their views and lived experiences, there were four themes they wanted me to share with you from a former player's point of view, so here we go. The first theme was *Football First*, the second was *Academics Second*, the third was *Teambuilding*, and the fourth was *Leadership Skills and Development*. When it came to football first, it was clear that they all felt that there was too much focus on football and a lack of focus on academics. All participants stated football came first, and for you to understand that football will always come first and will not change, so be prepared. They also expressed that as a college football player you have to prepare, compete, and improve in order to play on the field. Many believed that coaches and those associated with the football program will insist that you focus on the game of football 24/7. One participant explained that you will be evaluated yearly to justify reinstating your scholarship, so understand that you may not be signing a four-year scholarship but a year-to-year scholarship based on your play. As a result, all participants stated that you'll be required to become more focused on producing on the field, not realizing that if you're not focused in the classroom, you will become academically ineligible. Therefore, their advice to you is to become as balanced as a student-athlete as possible and not just a football player.

This is valuable information for you moving forward, because you now know that your coaches are going to put great emphasis on playing the game of football at the highest level. This is also beneficial information because it is understood that you'll need to consistently work out, learn the game, and become better at your craft to be reinstated so you can show your talents on the field. With such an emphasis on being prepared on the football field, I would encourage you to become a student of the game by studying your position, to include studying your opponent's tendencies as well as their strengths and weaknesses, if you want to become the best. Lastly, study those who played the position before you and those who are playing your position now, and research their work habits and mindset to the game. Following these key suggestions will definitely increase your odds of making your dreams become a reality!

The second theme expressed was *Academics Second*. Many communicated that their interest was solely in the game of football. Therefore, the majority of their preparation was to excel on the football field and not in the classroom. Because of such a mindset, these same former players wanted me to share with you that it's time to change your mindset and thought process. One participant shared that the academics for him was very challenging because there was no interest in the academic portion of school, to include feeling as though he was not prepared coming out of high school. This statement alone proves my earlier concept of ensuring that you choose the college or university that has a major closely related to what you like, along with playing the game of football. This is why I suggest that you should compare your high school academic scores to the schools that are recruiting you, to ensure you're not behind before you start.

Similar to the above statements, these former players wanted me to express that they had no idea of how to study, as well as possessing a lack of interested in the subjects offered. That was truly a telling point, hearing those comments, because I had just shared with you the need to ask for help when needed, as well as finding a major that fits your personality and interests. If you are like some who either don't know how to study or don't like it, start now by finding ways to do so.

As a start, I would begin with my teachers, counselors, and tutors for assistance. Sadly, many shared that in looking back, they were afraid to ask for help and didn't possess the overall GPA or SAT scores to even be accepted to that school. These same participants ended by stating that they were recruited because they played the game well, not because they were good students. In looking back, had they not been football players, they probably would not have been accepted as regular students, because their SAT scores and GPA were too low.

For those who shared that they weren't interested in academics, know that that's not good enough, because you will have to perform in the classroom regardless. This also goes back to my comments pertaining to how to choose the school that best suits you. Do you remember what I said? I basically said to think about what you like to do and to see if that school offers your interest as a major. By doing so, you'll perform at your highest and achieve in both football and your academics.

While discussing the theme pertaining to *Teambuilding/ Player*, the majority stated the game of football contributed to them becoming better leaders and team players in their personal and professional lives. Many shared that the same personal and professional issues football players endure now are very similar to what they endured while playing the game of football. Several expressed that they used previously learned lessons on the football field to adapt and relate to similar issues in their personal and professional lives. All of the participants indicated and wanted you to know that the best part of being a college football player was the relationship-building and long-lasting relationships that are established.

My question to you is: What does this mean to you? For me and hopefully for you, this means that the game of football, if played and studied the right way, will teach you a plethora of positive personal attributes. These gentlemen just spoke about teamwork and becoming great team-players, so please understand that in life, this is what it's all about, because you can't do it alone. If you run, throw, or catch for 100 yards, you didn't do it by yourself—you needed your teammates. If you get an A or B in a subject, you needed your instructor, a friend, a book, or a video to get you to that point. When you graduate and become employed by a company and later the manager or CEO, you'll need to possess the qualities of becoming a good team player as well as understanding the concept of teamwork in order to achieve success. Becoming a great teammate and team player isn't negotiable, it's a must!

The last thing these former players wanted me to share and communicate with you dealt with *Leadership Skills and Development*. First, let's define leadership. Leadership is the method whereby one individual influences other group members toward the attainment of a defined group or organizational goals. In the game of football, there are captains and co-captains, as well as starters and second-team players. When it comes to leadership, one of the former players expressed that the goal of every football player is to become a starter and/or captain. In both situations, you must lead by example on and off the football field in order to gain the trust of your teammates and others.

As one of the former players shared, he felt that way

because the game of football helped him to understand what it is like to be a leader. As a co-captain of the football team, he conveyed that he knew he had to become a hard worker, lead by example, and represent the team and himself at the highest level and in the most respectful way, as you'll need to do. Others demonstrated that becoming a leader on the football field was important individually and for the team. In the end, all participants mentioned that the game of football assisted with their leadership skills as well as their personal and professional development, and their wish is for the game of college football to assist you in the same way.

As stated in an earlier point, if you want to become a leader, you have to become a great team player and understand the concept of teamwork. So, what does this mean for you? This means that if you want to become considered a good leader, you can't skip curfew, you can't cheat, do drugs, get drunk, be disrespectful to others, or harm others in any kind of way. This also means that you must set a good example in the classroom as well as in your public service, just to name a few. Being a leader will say to others that you're also doing due diligence in the classroom, because if you don't, you won't be able to lead on the field. Leading others is a privilege and something that's earned. With that being said, let's put it all together in this last chapter and discuss what *life after football* is all about and how the game of football will prepare you for future endeavors.

Life After Football

LIFE AFTER FOOTBALL is simply the next chapter of your life, a life that will provide you with awesome opportunities of becoming a husband, a father, and one day a grandpa. In this new life, your personal and professional outcomes may become considerably different from others' due to choosing a path unrelated to your peers or because a certain path has chosen you. Life after football will be the changing of the guard because you will now have to switch roles and start making life decisions. Instead of your head coach and offensive coordinator drawing up plays and making your assignments, you will now start the process of taking over their role by doing the same. The difference is, your plays and assignments will become short-term, and long-term personal and professional goals and the assignments will be the steps to achieving those goals. As a result, your plays and assignments are going to be related to life and your well-being as a person and not football.

Despite taking ownership of the newfound tasks of having to draw up your own plays and make decisions, don't fret, because you will already have been equipped with the tools and lessons needed to become successful. The same tools that you'll already be equipped with will represent a culmination of all the years you have experienced on and off the field as a college football player, to include the good experiences with the bad. Just like you'll prepare to make plays on Saturdays, it will now be time to make plays as a man, every day of the week!

When it comes to being away from the game of football for the first time, it's going to feel awkward because your mind and your body will have been programmed to the on-field and classroom competition and not the competition of life. There may even be a bit of fear and unsettledness because you won't know what's next, including not knowing where to start. I can remember being home and asking myself, "What happens now?" For me, I didn't waste any time looking for a job. Looking for a job was my first alternative because I just wasn't mentally ready to tackle the school thing again. Though I knew I would eventually go back, looking for work and maintaining a job was most important to me.

After some months of looking for work, I finally got hired and started working for Savannah River Site. For those of you who don't know, Savannah River Site is a nuclear facility located in Aiken South Carolina. My title was a LSE which stood for a Limited Service Employee. Because of my lack of degree attainment, I started at minimum wage, which in 1988 was a whopping $5 an hour! But to be honest, it wasn't the pay that bothered me, it was the one question that was always mentioned and asked once those that I worked with found out I played football for Georgia Tech. You want to take a guess as to what that question was? Guess! You're correct! The follow-up question that was always mentioned would be, "So what did you get your degree in?" I would be like, *Dang! Here we go again.* The near trauma and disappointment of not graduating just seemed to follow me in conversation no matter what. To prove what I stated before, not possessing a degree meant to others that I was not ready for positions of leadership, but I did qualify for the basic positions. At this point, I was starting to face a little reality and see the importance of a college degree.

So, I worked at that position for maybe a year and soon applied for an in- house job paying $8 an hour as a GSO, which stood for a General Service Operator. I worked on the asphalt crew and our job was to tour the site, find roads that had holes, and then patch or fill them up with asphalt. At the end of the day, making $8 an hour wasn't bad because I was progressing as a man, doing things the right way, drawing up my own plays, and making my own decisions. I need for you to realize that sometimes in life, you don't have to start at the top to feel good about yourself. Though I wasn't at the top, I was starting to feel good about myself.

By now, I was a permanent employee at Savannah River Site and becoming more and more motivated to succeed. I began using good communication skills on the job as I did on the football field, as well as showing an understanding of the concept of teamwork and becoming a good team player. Because I started exhibiting some of what the game of football taught me, my co-workers and manager began making suggestions to me about applying for different jobs. As a result, I made a significant jump by accepting a job as a radiological control inspector. In this position, I was the one that monitored and measured the radiation and contamination in the areas where the workers worked. By accepting this job, I went from $8 an hour to $20 an hour. In 1990, this was a great living for someone who did not possess a college degree. Still, I knew possessing a degree would allow other doors to open.

By this time, I was ready to go back to school to rightfully claim what I should have gotten years earlier. So, I confirmed that my employer would match my tuition by 100%. Do you know what this meant? This meant that if I earned at least a *B* in every class, my employer would reimburse me 100% of what I had paid! I was like, *Wow*, because I'm thinking that I was once on scholarship not having to pay a dime, and now the same thing was happening again. This was truly a blessing and I wasn't about to mess it up!

In thinking back to the professional athletes we discussed in the last chapter, I too did as they did by going back to school, and so can you if you're one of the ones that don't walk out with a college degree. Again, not graduating with a degree isn't the end of the world, but not possessing one may make your climb to the top a little bit harder. Whatever road you take or whatever road is laid out for you, know that you can and will conquer. In case you forgot or may be unsure, here's why you will conquer!

As we all know, the term conquer simply means to overcome or take control of any given situation, person, place, or thing. Gentlemen, you will conquer in life after football because the game would have taught you how to become strong, to include becoming mentally and physically tough. Being mentally and physically tough will assist you in those times when you've had a long day at work and still have your duties and responsibilities at home. When that time comes, just remember those long practices and having to go back to the room and study. It's the same thing! The fact that you'll have to work around large groups of people from all walks of life won't be an issue for you either, and you'll conquer that, too.

You'll conquer and work well around others because you would have been taught to work well around others from playing the game of football. By this time, you would have had teammates from all walks of life, possessing many attitudes and ideas from different geographical areas. Remember, the key component that's going to make your transition of working with others easier is being a good team player and understanding the concept of teamwork. Understand that you will already have been taught and lived those concepts from your college football days, so you'll be ahead of others.

For me, the transition was easy because I made sure I applied every personal and professional situation to similar situations from what the game of football taught me. That's how powerful the game is, has been, and always will be for you. Playing the game of college football and going through the many personal experiences of playing the game will one day be your blueprint, along with the Holy Bible, to becoming a successful person both personally and professionally. Please understand that whether you make it to the NFL, don't make it to the NFL, obtain a degree, or don't obtain a degree, all will still apply as lessons learned.

The same will apply when you become a supervisor, manager, CEO, etc. Becoming one of the three means that you will be leading others in accomplishing the goals of your company. When that time comes, you will have to lead by example, showing leadership through excellence in and out of the office. Again, this won't be a problem for you, because being a former member of a football team means that you already possess an understanding of what it takes to lead others and to live in an exemplary way. At the end of the day, the ball will be in your court when it comes to becoming the best future versions of yourself as a father, husband, and someday grandpa.

Last, let's not waste valuable information that has been stored. So, what am I talking about when it comes to information being stored? What I'm talking about is making sure that you share what you've learned from playing college football and how the game of football has helped you in your life. One way to do this is to become a mentor in your community once your time in football is over. Becoming a mentor to young men coming behind you will show a great deal of unselfishness and care. Finally, becoming a mentor and sharing your story will show others how they can use their own experiences not only to grow in each aspect of their own lives but to help others realize their own potential and dreams. The sky is the limit for you, and I wish you the best in your future endeavors. God bless!

Recruiting 101 Points of Emphasis:

- The recruiting process is designed to obtain the best football players and not the best students!

- The recruiting process is designed to get you excited about playing the game of football for that university!

- During your recruiting process, you and your family will be treated like royalty, so don't become naïve, thinking you are the only one being treated that way!

- Very little time will be spent on the future of your academics so make sure you take the time to inquire about the variety of majors offered.

- Remember, on every recruiting trip, each school will share why they are the best choice for you from a football standpoint but not necessarily from an academic standpoint.

Recruiting 101 Chapter Questions:

- What are your favorite subjects?

- What are your academic goals?

- What are your athletic goals?

- What are your interests outside of football?

- What questions will you ask on your recruiting trips?

Dreams Versus Reality Points of Emphasis:

- When it comes to dreams, know that dreams do come true, so pursue your dreams like there's no tomorrow!

- The reality of the game of football is "next man up," so make sure you are prepared, mentally and physically!

- The reality is that only 2% of college football players get the opportunity to play the game of football on a professional level!

- The reality is that in the eyes of Corporate America, you are not prepared to hold leadership positions if you don't possess a college degree!

- The reality is that coaches are paid millions of dollars to win games with great players and not great students, so getting good grades and staying academically eligible is up to you!

Dreams Versus Reality Chapter Questions:

- What are your dreams when it comes to football?

- What are your dreams after your football career is over?

- What are you doing now and what will you do in the future to ensure you graduate with a college degree?

- What would you like your major to be while in college?

- What is your dream job aside from playing professional football?

Who Are You Listening To? Points of Emphasis:

- As a high school football player transitioning into college, understand that influences will come in many different forms!

- Research has shown that if you are a young man from a lower-class family whose parents have not graduated from college, you are less likely to promote working hard in the classroom. Regardless, you can succeed academically!

- Because you may be a football player who comes from a middle to upper- class family with at least one parent who possesses a college degree, know that you are not exempt from academic failure.

- Dismiss the negative comments that you may hear pertaining to your capabilities of performing at a high level on the field and in the classroom!

- Regardless, know that you have options beyond playing the game of football!

Who Are You Listening To? Chapter Questions:

- What are your options beyond football?

- Are the individuals you're listening to only promoting football, or are they promoting academics too?

- Are you working toward being successful at things other than football? If so, what are those things, and what steps do you believe are needed to ensure success?

- Who are your *negative* critics? Do you believe these individuals are good for you, and if not, what do you believe you should do?

- Who are you *positive* critics? Do you believe these individuals are good for you, and if so, what do you believe you should do?

The Truth Shall Set You Free Chapter Points of Emphasis:

- Statistics have proven that there's a lack of graduation rates among football players, specifically Black football players.

- In Division 1 football programs, football generally comes first!

- In Division 1 football programs, academics generally comes second!

- Coaches are paid millions of dollars to win on the football field, not to graduate students!

- Certain nationalities are grouped into the same major, which is normally the easiest of majors to include the lowest paid once leaving college!

The Truth Shall Set You Free Chapter Questions:

- What will you do now that you are aware of the low graduation rates among college football players?

- What will you do since you are aware that some colleges have poorer graduation rates than others?

- What is your plan to ensure that you are not in the percentage of football players who do not graduate?

- What is your plan to ensure that you are in the 2% of college football players who play professionally?

- What motivates you, and how will this motivation help you achieve your goals?

About the Author

DR. ROOSEVELT ISOM, Jr., better known as "Bug" Isom in the football world, is a former George P. Butler High School standout and former wide receiver for the Georgia Tech Yellow Jackets. As a high school football player, "Bug" Isom won numerous awards, such as Male Athlete of the Year, Most Valuable Player, and Player of the Week. He was also a Top 30 Prospect in the State of Georgia who started as a defensive back in the Georgia North/South Allstar Game. "Bug" holds the longest run from scrimmage at his former high school and holds the second-longest run from scrimmage in the county's history. Further, "Bug" was the regional champ in track and field for two consecutive years in the 100, 200, 4X100, and 4X400. Because of such success, "Bug" was highly recruited and sought after by a plethora of schools that included Georgia Tech, Georgia, Georgia Southern, South Carolina, Clemson, Furman, Mississippi State, Tennessee, Purdue, and as far out as UCLA. Consequently, "Bug" had the pleasure of visiting a lot of schools and meeting a wide variety of coaches and players during the recruiting process. Many now describe "Bug" as an expert on this process due to his lived experiences and doctoral research. From an academic standpoint, "Bug" is the author of a published dissertation titled

"PERSONAL READINESS FOR LEADERSHIP:
A PHENOMENOLOGICAL STUDY OF
BLACK FORMER NCAA FOOTBALL PLAYERS."

"Bug's" dissertation validates a lot of what's discussed in his new book pertaining to why football players are prepared for personal readiness on the football field and not in the classroom. *3rd & 10/Overcoming the Pitfalls of Becoming a College Football Player* is his first book.

Roosevelt "Bug" Isom

GEORGIA TECH

1984 **1987**

CPSIA information can be obtained
at www.ICGtesting.com
Printed in the USA
FSHW011634191220
76862FS